This book is dedicated to n encouraged me to write it, and kept some of the stories alive. Also to our six children, in age order: Joy, Nicky, Liz, Chris, Jenny and Josh, all of whom suffered the regime of my school and survived!

Author's note

If it helps, you can think of this as a work of fiction, or you may prefer to consider it as an accurate account, but in truth it falls between the two. Every character, whether adult or child is a real person, but some names have been changed to preserve anonymity and some are more than one character morphed into a single one. Ninety-eight per cent of the events are based on reality but there have been many embellishments and a lot of literary licence to help the book along.

It has been written as a daily journal to bring characters and stories to a cohesive whole, but to do this the timescale has been contracted into one year. Most of it is based on what happened in one school, but some stories from other schools have been drafted in. In the journal, which goes from January to December, a row of asterisks at the end of a chapter denotes a gap in the entries.

A big thank you to everyone who came through my schools for helping to provide the content, and particularly those who have reminded me of events I had forgotten. I hope all your memories are as happy as mine. If you recognise yourself in the pages, I won't tell if you don't!

Enjoy!

David Watterson

1

The snow continued to fall lightly on the school playground. Although the two centimetre depth was beginning to get deeper, it wasn't enough to close the school. Which was just as well considering it was my first day at the school – my first day as a head teacher. Closing would not have been a good start. I looked around the old Victorian classroom that doubled as a hall. There is a lot of work to be done to make it look like we are no longer in Victorian times. I dusted the snow off my coat and hung it in the four square metre room that is my office, the staffroom and the school office.

I heard a rattling at the big, ancient back door. The first pupils were arriving with a parent in tow. With a heavy clunk, the door slowly swung inwards, rusty hinges creaking. Two boys burst through the opening, scattering snow across the classroom floor. They were followed by a flat-capped head poking around the door.

"Come in out of the snow," I called.

The middle-aged man (was he an older dad or a younger grandad?) appeared, shaking snow from his country overcoat.

"It's c....c....cold out there," he said, feigning chattering teeth.

"Y....y....yes it is," I replied, playing the game.

"We're in for even m....m....more snow this afternoon," he continued.

"Well let's hope we d....d....don't have to shut the sc....sc....school," was my reply.

Five minutes into the conversation it began to dawn on me that this poor guy had a debilitating stammer, and I'd spent the last five minutes making fun of him.

"By the way, I'm David," I said. "I'm sorry, I didn't mean to take the michael."

"I'm Michael," he said, holding out his hand.

It's been a strange first day!

* * * * * * * * * * * * * * *

2

Despite the awkward start, the last two weeks have gone quite smoothly. The snow persisted, and as one of my maxims is 'children learn more if they have fun', there were plenty of snowball fights and snowmen to be built. Finally, now the snow is a metre deep on the road at the front of the school, I have had to close it. My car ran into a drift a quarter of a mile from the school so I abandoned it to walk in and telephone around. Not that it really mattered; only three or four of the children live within walking distance. I have discovered that the village is spread out over several miles with many isolated properties. Any I couldn't reach would have to turn back anyway.

On my own in the school today I have been able to reflect on the last couple of weeks, and Sheila, the cleaner/caretaker is going to be a problem. She moans about everything!

I have been able to plan the future of the school year – The Development Plan. What strengths have I got that I can nurture in the children in my care? Music and Drama are high on my list, so there will be plenty of those, and with only fifty pupils they will all be able to be involved. I think we'll make this pantomime year. We can perform one a term; Jack & the Beanstalk, Cinderella and Aladdin will be good ones to do, and I'll write my own scripts to suit my cast. I'll also throw in a mini-musical at some point.

Residential trips are a specialism of mine so we'll squeeze in a couple of those. Sport, I've never been good at, but is so important in school, so games will focus on the fun aspect. There is no sign of a Health & Safety manual in school, so maybe one hasn't been written yet, which is good news for me.

The only other thing to think about is Ofsted. I'm sure we are due an inspection this year, so I'll be ready for that. Or not!

* * * * * * * * * * * * * * *

3

The school field is leased from the smallholding next door. To reach it we have to leave the bottom of the playground by a gate into their property, then walk through the grounds to the field. Living at the property are two elderly parents and their two Neanderthal sons aged twelve and fourteen. Then there's the dog! The creature is a vicious, slavering, foaming, teeth-baring wild animal which longs to sink its teeth into an adult calf muscle, or in the case of skinny children, to gnaw on a shin bone. The path to the field is littered with the gruesome remains of headless chickens, the work of either the dog or the cave boys. Fortunately the dog is usually tethered, but the lead is long. Whenever anyone goes through the gate, the dog comes flying out of hiding and tears towards them, teeth bared, flecks of spittle and foam flying, a deep growling erupting from its throat, and as it reaches maximum speed it is yanked backwards by the chain attached to its collar.

This is fine – until today! Today it was loose. Fortunately we knew this before playtime because the mongrel had come through the unlatched gate and was stalking the empty playground. Being unable to contact the house owners I decided to call the police. After an indoor play, a policeman turned up on his bike. He's the youngest policeman I've ever seen, which is probably why he was on a bike. I explained the situation to PC Just Out of Nappies.

"We'll go round the house, then," he naively said.

I was unhappy with the word 'we', but I selected a yard brush with sharp bristles as a defensive weapon and offered a similar one to him.

"Nah, I'll be fine," he assured me.

Together we approached the house from the road at the front. All was quiet for the first thirty seconds, then all hell broke loose. Our nemesis came tearing towards us in total excitement at the sight of four adult shanks to go at. Seeing the snarling, salivating beast heading full-pelt towards us, PC Just Out of Nappies froze and yelled,

"Give me that brush!"

The chances of that happening were zilch – the brush was mine!

"On yer bike!" I replied.

I backed off towards the road, cleaning the Hound of the Baskervilles' bared teeth with the yard broom bristles. As I reached the road, it turned on its tail and loped disappointedly back to its hiding place. I looked around to find the young policeman had taken me literally, and was pedalling away into the distance. Hopefully things will be back to normal tomorrow.

4

Today was exciting; I took two dead foxes into school. I'd found them at the side of the road on the way to school. Apart from broken legs they were intact. I suspect they had been mating in the middle of the road. I deduced that from the way their legs were broken and the smile on their faces. Obviously this was not discussed with the children, but it was great for them to see, touch and study these wild animals in the middle of the classroom floor. At the end of the day we dug a large grave at the top of the field and buried them both there. R.I.P.

A new little lad called Jimmy and his older brother, Mark, have started today. I think we will have problems. Jimmy was swearing profusely and he's only four years old. I had a word with his mum about it at the end of school. She was really upset and said, "I don't know where the little bugger gets it from!"

Anyway, there's no doubt in my mind.

We have got an early start rehearsing the first panto of the year. We are going to do Cinderella. All of the school is involved. A third of the classroom is taken up with a stage which a parent has cleverly designed and constructed for us. I've built a chimney breast and fireplace out of hardboard, and erected a narrow P.E. bench behind it, accessible by a step-ladder which is just below the ceiling. It is the entry point for the Fairy Godmother who will slide down it to miraculously appear on stage in the fireplace. Amanda is very nervous about coming down it, especially with a wand in her hand. We'll video it before we finally perform, which should be fun. Hopefully none of the governors will notice the six-inch nails that I have hammered into the wooden floor to support the structure.

* * * * * * * * * * * * *

5

Today was a good day for sport. I wanted it to be fun so I invented a game. It is quite simple really; there are hardly any rules. The aim is to score a goal with a ball, which has to go in the front of the goal. There are no nets on the goals up the field, so the children can run in from the back and then back through the front. Genius! The ball may be propelled in any way whatsoever, such as kick, throw, carry, stuff it up your shirt, etc. The opposition can retrieve the ball in almost any way. The one rule is not to deliberately cripple another child. There are no boundaries, either. The field is bordered by deep Lincolnshire dykes, sometimes full of water. If the ball goes in, the first child in after it is obviously at an advantage. If the ball goes out of the school premises into the farmer's crops, the game continues on the understanding that it comes back at the earliest chance. Picking up the opposition member who has the ball and running with both into the goal will, I think, be a popular move. Today the game was a resounding success, but I don't think Sheila will like the mud! We ended the lesson with a competition to name the game. The winner was 'Exhaustiball' because they were all worn out. My own suggestion of 'Anarchy' was met with vacant stares.

During the afternoon we started to film scenes from Cinderella prior to tomorrow's first performance. Amanda was still nervous about coming down the chute, so we tried giving her a hands-free attempt and then someone tossing her wand on to the stage over the chimney breast. She managed the entrance well but the wand-thrower was not so successful. Four times it appeared and then disappeared without landing on stage. Amanda was in fits of laughter. When there was finally a successful throw, it bounced off Cinderella's head. It will make some good outtakes at the end of the video. However, we hope all will run smoothly on the night.

Then Sue came in to help me teach the children to waltz. It's important if the ballroom scene is to look effective. The couples with lines to say have to make sure they're centre front to deliver them. It's not an easy thing for children to learn, unless they've been for dancing lessons already.

6

The L.E.A. local schools' inspector telephoned to introduce herself this morning as she's new to the job. I've heard that heads call her 'The Dragon Lady'. We didn't get off to a good start; one of her first questions was, "What's your role?"

I thought – 'Silly woman, what does she think I do?' I said, "I'm a teaching head."

There was a pause at the other end. "No," she said. "What's your role?"

"I'm a head teacher with a teaching commitment," I added by way of explanation, thinking, 'What's she on?'

Another pause. Then I could feel heat coming down the phone and almost smell the smoke.

"No....," she breathed heavily; "What's your roll? R..O..L..L!

A pause this time at my end while I prepared to say, "Cheese and tomato if you're offering."

Fortunately she spoke before I had time. She spoke slowly and emphatically. "How many children do you have on the school roll?"

"Oh...." I said. "Fifty."

It was a great relief when the conversation ended. She's going to come to a governors' meeting to see us in person. I can't wait!

The first performance of Cinderella mainly went well tonight. The audience were sat in the two-thirds of the room not taken up by the stage. We have borrowed special lighting from a local Secondary School – a strobe and ultra-violet light for special effects. Explosions always go down well. Stage maroons come in three sizes – small, medium and large. The large ones are for huge theatres and auditoriums, so they would be perfect for our little classroom!

I've given myself a small role in it – lead by example – as a castle servant in an attic scene. Buttons takes the servants to the haunted attic for the night, and the scene is set for a bit of fun. A monstrous spider was lowered over the backdrop using a fishing rod. After the usual shouting from the audience, the plan was for me to unhook the spider and then we throw it around to each other in panic. Unfortunately the spider got stuck on the hook, and when I finally got it off, the hook went into my finger. Thinking all was well, the backstage girl wound in the fishing line. My finger went up with it until it broke through the skin. I tried to stop it bleeding all over stage but the audience found it hilarious. After all, it is a panto; it's meant to be funny.

Oh no it's not!

7

We've begun to plan the first of two residential trips for this year. This one will be a late winter/early spring camping trip on a canvas-covered barge. The summer term trip will probably be more of an adventure one. There is plenty of interest for the days on the barge.

The second performance of Cinderella today was not without problems. There was no repeat of yesterday's fishing hook problem, but when the ghost came in to haunt us, covered in the obligatory white sheet, there was a shout from a little pre-school lad in the audience – "It's Ben!" However much we tried to convince him that it was a ghost, he insisted throughout the scene that it was Ben. We either hadn't got the costume perfected, (I think he may have noticed the watch on his wrist and the shiny shoes,) or he had inside information, because it was, in fact, Ben.

Tom, a really good young actor, has been playing the part of the dame in the panto. He was brilliant today, and improvised well when his wig accidentally fell off. The really clever part of the panto was the conversion of a pumpkin into a splendid coach. Behind a back curtain the coach awaited, with fairy lights all round it. The plan was as follows: the Fairy Godmother spins in a strobe light, casting her spell; on the magic word, one back-stage lighting 'technician' child switches off the strobe; another presses the electricity switch to activate the explosion; a third switches on the fairy lights and three others drop the backcloth so that the coach magically appears. I was lying on my back at the side of the stage, out of sight. My job was to surreptitiously make the pumpkin disappear. The moment came. There was an earth-shattering explosion as the auditorium maroon let rip, temporarily deafening everyone in the room. The cast was ready for this experience after yesterday's performance. The lighting all went according to plan and I grabbed the pumpkin and brought it down on to my chest. I must have done it with more force than yesterday because it was at this point that I realised I should have had a fresh pumpkin and not one several months old. The casing burst and there was a nauseating smell as the foul insides of the pumpkin soaked into my shirt.

The panto was a resounding success, my bleeding finger from yesterday and my stinking shirt tonight being the only casualties. As they left, the audience of parents, friends and governors was chattering loudly and prodding at their ears, but they gave the head teacher a wide berth for some reason.

I was pleased that Ofsted were not there!

* * * * * * * * * * * * * *

8

The camping barge trip is now over and we have had a meeting with parents tonight to celebrate our safe return yesterday. The canvas-covered barge we rented left a lot to be desired. During the winter these barges chug up and down the canal carrying a cargo of coal. Then in mid-March they are converted for sleeping in bunk beds. As we arrived at the canal side we realised that we had a chosen a bad week. The first week of the barges as camping pods coincided with the coldest week we've had all winter. There was no heating on the boat and I went to bed in pyjamas, clothes on top, including a jumper and I slept in a mountain sleeping bag. I was still cold, and as I walked between the bunk beds I wasn't sure if the children were alive or had died of hyperthermia. We got up on the first morning to a frozen canal. The water we had left in saucepans overnight was ice and our shoes were frozen to the decking.

We did get moving, but at one lock Anthony stepped backwards off the quayside and into the canal. Fortunately it was only three feet deep there and he didn't want to get out because he said it was warmer in.

The next day George had also been in the water because whilst on the canal bank he kicked a stone and his shoe shot into the air and landed in the middle of the canal. As the water wasn't deep I told him to take his trousers off and fetch it, which he did.

During the meeting tonight we showed pictures of the trip to the parents. The only complaint that George's mum had was that he was still wearing the same underpants that he went in. I thought it better not to tell her that they had probably been frozen to his backside!

* * * * * * * * * * * * *

9

The toilet arrangements at the school are rather primitive; the toilet block is at the bottom of the playground. The boys are at one end of the block and the girls at the other. The one staff toilet is the first one in on the girls' side so I try to go as infrequently as possible. There are no washing facilities there and the relieved customers have to return to school and remember to wash their hands. There is no heating either, so in the really cold days at the beginning of term I had to be in early to defrost the cisterns in order to keep the school open. This morning the children were out on the playground looking for their teacher, Mrs. Jones.

"Maybe she's in the loo," said a little voice.

One girl climbed up on to the back of another and peered through the frosted glass.

"Yes, she's in there," she said.

I thought it was time for improvements, so at this afternoon's head teachers' meeting with the council, L.E.A. bigwigs, etc., there was an opportunity. About a hundred head teachers were listening to the Chairman of the County Council and the Chairman of the Education Committee patting themselves on the back about their plans for I.T. development in school offices and the amount of taxpayers' money they would spend on it.

After a boring hour during which I only dozed off twice, I was awoken by,

"Any questions from the head teachers present?"

I grabbed my chance and stood up to ask, "Office computers are all well and good, but what about money for schools with outside loos with no heating or washing facilities, where four year-olds have to put coats, hats and wellies on in all weathers to go and have a wee, not to mention staff's frozen assets?"

There was a tumbleweed moment in the room; one of those rare moments when councillors are speechless. Eventually the Chairman of the County Council spoke.

"I thought we had solved that problem twenty years ago," he mumbled.

I gave my name and the name of the school.

"We'll be in touch," was the reply.

"And pigs might fly, which would make the price of bacon rise," I thought.

But didn't say!

10

Jimmy was under a table today and wouldn't come out. After ten unsuccessful minutes a distraught Mrs. Jones appeared in my classroom to tell me. I walked into Jimmy's classroom, and in my most authoritative voice boomed,

"Jimmy! Out!"

Jimmy shot out like a bullet from a gun. I turned and went back to my classroom, trying to hide the smirk. Oh, the power!!

I acquired a puppet recently and thought I would try out my skill of ventriloquism today. He's a good size, and similar to a proper ventriloquist's dummy. He's got red hair and looks mischievous. I've called him Gus. He's disobedient and downright rude. The children love him! I'm going to have some fun; I'll be able to get away with all sorts of misdemeanours. Gus will be to blame, not me!

A delivery arrived today from ESPO, the company we order stock from. Amongst other ordinary things, like pencils, were 10,000 salary envelopes. We don't use salary envelopes here, but if we did I have worked out that the supply would last us 200 years. Seventeen large boxes, each containing 500 envelopes were piled into our tiny corridor. We can just get through the door.

"We've run out," said the delivery man. "The other three boxes will arrive when they're in stock."

He wouldn't take them back. I've investigated and it seems that one perspex ruler has the same order number as a box of 500 salary envelopes, and I ordered twenty rulers. I'm not surprised they're now out of stock. Maybe we can do some construction work with the boxes in craft lessons. Perhaps re-create the Great Wall of China for instance.

My favourite spelling mistake of all time today. Margaret was supposed to be writing 'public library' in her story, but actually wrote 'pubic library'. I opened my mouth to comment on the queues there would be outside, but thought better of it.

11

The Chair of Governors' wife came in today with a present in a bag. They are farmers and obviously understand wildlife.

"We shot a rabbit last night," she said cheerfully.

I didn't say anything in the pause. Then she spoke again.

"It was pregnant."

Pause. I think she expected me to know where the conversation was headed.

"The foetus is in the skin sac in the bag," she contributed.

My face was twisting slightly but no words were coming out of my mouth.

"Thought you might like to cut it open and show the children."

She plonked it on the desk, turned and left. I still hadn't said anything.

"Thanks!" I called to the closing door.

So all the children were sat round me as I had the 'scalpel' poised above the sac.

"Are you ready to see the baby rabbit?" I said. "Sadly, it won't be alive."

That sounded better than 'It's dead!'

They nodded and I pierced the sac. The worst smell that I have ever experienced seeped out and began to fill the room. Inside the sac looked nothing at all like a foetus. She'd given me its stomach! We all headed for the door and fresh air. Several children were retching; all were holding their noses.

They had an extended playtime while I went in to dispose of the offending organ. Sheila won't be best pleased.

So as I thought earlier: Farmers understand wildlife!!

12

There was a football match at the end of school this afternoon. For a tiny school we are doing remarkably well. We beat another school 14-0 in a half-hour game. It's all down to David and Claire, my best two players. They are wizards. Claire, one of the few girl players in the league at the moment, tears off down the left wing with the ball at her feet, then instinctively knowing where David is, crosses to him. He either volleys or heads it in. This happens systematically every two minutes. You would think that the opposition would notice what is happening and try to stop them. They were lucky to get nil!

After the match, Sheila was up in arms as usual; she'd just cleaned the cloakroom when the players got in from the field. I told her if there was no muck she wouldn't have a job. That didn't go down well! Heaven help us, it's clay work in craft tomorrow, and that creates the biggest mess ever.

Today I've ordered an incubator for hatching chicks and ducklings which we are going to keep in the classroom for three weeks so that we can weigh and measure them daily. I'm anticipating that muck and smells will be at a premium then.

Our school's inspector came tonight for a routine chat at the governors' meeting, as promised. She's a fearful sight – about fifty years old, hair swept into a bun, sharp features and eyes that you keep expecting to light up red. She dresses to kill in a knee-length crimson skirt split high up the thigh and lipstick to match. But what really catches the eye are the earrings. Each one is a silver dragon that hangs an inch from her lobes and swings mesmerizingly backwards and forwards. The earrings are probably what gave her the nickname 'The Dragon Lady'. But they also say everything about her personality!

Poor Matthew, an elderly farmer and local council-appointed governor was sat directly in front of her at the governors' meeting. Within five minutes he was in a trance-like state. The combination of swaying earrings and split skirt had worked its magic. His eyes had glazed over, his jaw had dropped and his tongue was beginning to hang out.

Of course, it could all just have been the excitement of attending a governors' meeting!

* * * * * * * * * * * * * *

13

Science today was about unequal forces. It's really a very basic primary concept even though it sounds complicated. I had a brilliant plan. We cleared the classroom of tables and chairs and set up a tug-of-war rope down the centre. The plan was to have a couple of goes with children fairly balanced on each side, then to prove a point I would join in and go head-to-head with one child, and obviously easily win.

The first two contests went well – lots of shouting and cheering and teams struggling to win.

"Now....," I said. "I need a volunteer to pull against me."

Beth's hand shot up first, and without thinking, I instinctively picked her. Beth is the biggest Y6 I have ever seen; tall and solidly built. Out of school she could have passed for a fifteen year-old. She flexed her muscles and picked up her end of the rope. Now a little apprehensive I picked up mine. As soon as she started to tug I knew I was in trouble. I dug in my heels, leaned back and heaved. Nothing! Beth increased her pulling power, and at that moment I knew I was going to lose.

I immediately aborted the contest as I knew it would not prove the point I was trying to make. At least, that's the excuse I gave myself. I've learnt what I should already know – test out your experiments and hypotheses before presenting them in class!

Well, the Easter holiday now looms; tomorrow will be the last day of term. Hopefully everyone will have a well-deserved break and return refreshed for the summer term.

■■■

14

The new term started today, and we made an early start on our next production – Aladdin. The stage was put back up over the holiday, and it has a labyrinth of tunnels underneath it, with a concealed entrance to them from the stage itself. A huge laundry basket with no bottom covers the hole. The plan is for a dozen children to pile into the basket one at a time and just disappear. It's going to be great fun. If Jimmy disappears from his classroom, we'll know where to look.

We started the term's sport with a game of Exhaustiball. It went really well. Chris literally threw himself into it as usual, and got injured as usual! He made a meal of it, of course, as he often does so I've not sent a note home.

The incubator was set up today, and by the end of school it was up to heat, so the duck eggs have been put in and are now 'cooking'. They need longer than the hen eggs so they will go in later. Everyone is 'eggcited'.

15

It turns out that Chris had a broken collarbone yesterday. It's good that no-one's written a Health and Safety manual yet; I think that Exhaustiball would be banned.

Rehearsals for Aladdin went well today. I feel that crawling around in tunnels beneath the stage is less dangerous than sliding down a narrow bench from the ceiling. Amanda will be pleased that she hasn't got to repeat that type of stunt. The children have really enjoyed it. I've acquired smoke pellets for when the washing machines supposedly catch fire, and to make the magic lantern more effective when the genie appears.

I'm still waiting for the L.E.A. to get in touch about the provision of a new toilet block. I don't think they will and I'm hatching a plan! As well as ducks, and soon, chickens.

* * * * * * * * * * * * *

16

Today was a bit of a disaster! We did our rehearsal for the production, and being a panto there's some falling over in the slapstick scenes. I thought it would be a good idea to demonstrate how to fall over without getting hurt. However, I've never actually achieved this in my own experiences on stage. I also wrongly thought that it would be fun to demonstrate with a 'how not to do it' first with a comedy fall. I would follow this by saying,

"That's not how to do it, you could hurt yourselves."

Then I would hopefully show them a safer way. So the children were all gathered, eager to learn some new acting skills.

My memory of the event is still hazy. I do remember looking out of the back of the ambulance at a sea of young faces staring through the playground railings. Apparently there had been enthusiastic applause to begin with. Eventually, our teaching assistant, Mrs. Fuller, had raised the alarm and the ambulance had been called.

Most of this I have learned from a telephone call at home after my discharge. It seems I have to take a couple of days off until I'm sure there's no more permanent damage from the concussion.

Thank goodness Ofsted weren't in today!

* * * * * * * * * * * * * * *

17

So back in school today following two days off, I faced the same group of children and said,

"So that's not how to do it – you could hurt yourselves!"

The rest of the rehearsal went without a hitch. Paul is a confident young actor; I've chosen him to be on stage on his own and to ad lib an audience song with the relatives and other friends that come along. It'll be a good experience for him.

Mrs. Tester has rehearsed the songs with them all in my absence. She has arthritic fingers but does really well playing the piano considering the problems she encounters.

Sheila was totally distraught after school tonight. She said she has had a break-in at home and some valuables were stolen. It sounds like she has adequate insurance to cover it all so it should be ok but it is very upsetting at the time.

The eggs should all be hatching in a few days.

Still nothing from the L.E.A. about the toilets!

TV-am are running a show called *Top Banana* in which children compete in a variety of challenges, a bit like *'It's a Knockout'*. I thought it would be good if we could compete. We've been accepted and will be travelling to Bristol to film it next week.

* * * * * * * * * * * * * * *

18

The performance of Aladdin went well today. I particularly enjoyed shoving foam pies into the children's faces when they opened the washing machine doors. The foam looked effective as the machines broke down and caught fire. The smoke pellets worked well to complete the illusion. Fortunately no smoke alarms went off, so I need to remember to check if there are any actually fitted.

The basket on stage was replaced by a cardboard rock to hide the hole to the tunnels for the genie scene. I crawled into the tunnels and below the hole in order to drop a lighted smoke pellet into Aladdin's lamp. The smoke poured out of the lamp, and the genie appeared with a loud bang. With the extra-large maroon the explosion was its usual powerful self. Most people's ears were back to normal by the end of the performance.

The best bit for me was Paul's audience song. He was amazing, getting the audience stirred up to sing along. He pointed to me at the piano and said,

"And at the piano is Mr. Watterson; not as good as Elton John, but better than Mrs. Tester!"

I'll take it as a compliment.

19

We packed away the stage this morning so the classroom is getting back to normal. I thought we'd try shinty today in games. It's like hockey but more exciting. There are no height restrictions on the swinging of the shinty stick. I've done the health and safety talk and told the children not to be behind someone when they swing the stick. I've also shown them how they can turn the stick the other way up to make a walking stick if accidents do happen. It's only a matter of time!

I've prepared and sent out my toilet block letters; fifty in all, to everyone that matters. That is the whole L.E.A. Education Committee, the Chairman of the County Council. L.E.A. inspectors and our local M.P. The letter said 'If you had to sit on these toilets, you'd soon do something about it.' I eagerly await responses.

I was tempted to use salary envelopes to send the letters in, then I would have been down to a mere 9,950!

The chickens and ducks have started hatching. The plan is to house them in the classroom for three weeks, measuring and weighing them every day to compare their growth rates. Everyone is fascinated at the shells being chipped open, the soggy yellow balls emerging, and in an hour looking cute and fluffy.

* * * * * * * * * * * * * *

20

We went to Bristol yesterday to compete in *Top Banana*. It was a long, long way to go and come back in a day, but we had an amazing time. The whole school went on a coach. All the children will get to see themselves on the tele; they're very excited. We were given a huge crate of bananas to come back with. The local newspaper knows we were going, so we can expect a report next week. The children feel like TV stars already.

Sheila's not in today; it turns out that she faked the break-in as an insurance scam and is awaiting sentencing. She certainly acted the broken-hearted victim well. I must remember to give her a part in the next panto. If she's not on holiday at Her Majesty's Pleasure!

Jimmy's brother, Mark, did a runner just before the end of school today. He was reported to be halfway round the village in a field across a dyke. With ten minutes to parents arriving, I jumped in my car to go and fetch him back. I imagine that his parents turning up to collect him, and me saying,

"We're not sure where he is – last seen in a field across a dyke!" would not go down well.

Fortunately I was able to retrieve him with seconds to spare.

All the chicks have now hatched; we've weighed and measured them all and set up a corner of the classroom as a pen. It's going to be fun!

Later in the afternoon we opened up the shells of the ones that didn't hatch. It was a brilliant educational experience to see the different stages of each foetus. We don't know why they died. I'm glad I had the foresight to undertake this outside; the smell was unbelievable.

* * * * * * * * * * * * *

21

It's a Sex Education discussion this week for the older children. Letters have been sent to parents informing them of this and advising that they can withdraw children from the lessons if they want. The aim is to be as open as possible, to discuss puberty and what to expect from their bodies, and to encourage questions both at home and in the school sessions.

Responses have begun to come in from my fifty letters about the toilets. Every phone call, letter or e-mail has so far said,

'We have sent your letter to Mr. Cook who is in charge of capital expenditure.'

Mr Cook, of course, had his own letter from me, so he'll be making a collection of them. The local M.P. has also told me that he has asked the L.E.A. what they are going to do for the school now, and for the future. The pressure is on.

The next residential trip is in the planning stages. The weather has warmed up of course, and we are avoiding canals. It will be an adventure trip with some exciting activities being organised.

22

The Sex Education discussion today proved interesting. Martin said he'd asked his dad what sexual intercourse was. I asked him to tell us his dad's reply. Martin replied that his dad had clouted him round the ear!

I'd forgotten that Samantha has a problem with blood; she goes weak at the sight of it. I was talking about periods when there was an almighty crash. Samantha, who had apparently been gripping her table tightly, had passed out, taking the table and chair with her. They were all in a heap on the floor.

"Ok," I said to the class, "this is where we put our First Aid training into practice. We'll put her in the recovery position." She soon came round and we quickly moved on to avoid the subject of blood.

We had another go at shinty this afternoon. Unfortunately Graham forgot the advice of not standing behind the stick-swinger. The teeth knocked out are not mendable, and he will probably have to wait until he's finished growing to have some false ones fitted. Samantha was quickly blindfolded to avoid a repeat of the morning's collapse.

Most toilet block replies have now come in. They have continued to be sent to Mr. Cook. I'm amused to think that there is a massive pile of identical letters on his desk. I've not yet had a reply from Mr. Cook.

23

Following the success of the dead foxes, I took a dead owl into school today. I found it on the grass verge near my house this morning. It's in perfect condition - apart from being dead, of course! The children stroked the soft feathers and studied it closely. I've been in touch with a taxidermist in a nearby village and offered it to him if we can have any pellets returned; that way we can look at what it has eaten.

I've heard from Mr. Cook! He was not a happy bunny. He said he's coming to see me. I'll look forward to that!

During morning break a stone came smashing through the staffroom window from the playground. Jimmy had got carried away and thrown it at someone, but his aim was terrible. We managed to clean up all the glass that was scattered across the room, but worst of all we had to throw our coffees away. Jimmy is now grounded at playtimes for several days.

* * * * * * * * * * * * * *

24

Another great day for football. After a 10-0 win against another small school we are third in the league and through to the quarter-finals of the cup tournament. One of the biggest schools in the area are playing us in the cup at the weekend. I can't wait.

The smell in the room from the ducks and chicks is building up. The classroom walls at the side of the pen are getting plastered with poo. I think we'll need to redecorate when they've gone.

Andrew seems to live in a world of his own. No-one plays with him in the playground. He often puts on a strange sort of walk – ducking one shoulder down and then standing back up; repeat. I asked him today what he was doing.

"Riding my bike," was the reply.

I was still mystified, but then at the end of the day I was at the school gate as the parents were arriving to collect their children. Andrew's dad was walking down the road using the same shoulder-ducking walk.

"Nice day for cycling!" I commented as he passed.

With a strange glance at me he continued into the playground without a word.

25

Sheila's back; she got community service and kept her job. The new, unbelievable stench of duck and chicken poo and urine hit her as she entered school. She took one look at the splattered walls and almost went into anaphylactic shock. I got the impression that a prison sentence now looked the more attractive proposition. At the end of school we cleared it all out. A local farm has had the chicks and ducklings. It was a brilliant exercise that covered both science and maths as we compared the relative weights and wingspans. It has been a good project but we'll have to redecorate soon. Next week is Sat's week. We are all looking forward to that!

We've had a competition to design a shirt as a school's P.E./Games uniform. One of the generous parents, whose business is supplying clothing, has offered to give all the children a polo shirt free of charge, and we supply the design for it. Jake did an excellent design and won the competition today. We will send this off and hopefully the shirts will be here in time for sports days at the end of term.

* * * * * * * * * * * * * *

26

Sat's have gone well this week. It began with a Sat's inspector turning up. Apparently they randomly come into some schools to check that there is no cheating; that papers are still sealed up and the tests are run according to the rules. The papers were, of course, still sealed; it's at least a sackable offence if they are not.

The interesting test was the practical science for Year 2. It was a floating and sinking experiment. The children had some objects and a bowl of water. They had to predict which objects would float and which would sink, and then try out their hypotheses. It was straightforward until they got to the tomato. It didn't sit on the top of the water, nor did it go to the bottom of the bowl, but hung below the surface. Teachers for a long time to come will probably be debating whether the tomato had floated or sunk, but Jessica had it sorted. She stuck her finger into the suspended tomato, making a hole big enough to make sure that it did sink. I think that initiative is worth a pass anyway.

I like the way children don't fail in Sat's. If they don't get Level One, they are working towards it. Matthew is struggling with reading; we've had to assess him as Working Towards the Bookcase. He'll get there eventually.

* * * * * * * * * * * * * *

27

The Year 6's have taken to singing and dancing in the classroom when it's a wet break time. They know all the actions to the latest pop songs and stand in a line to perform, so it's their equivalent of line dancing. It makes for an enjoyable break for them when they can't be outside. I join in when I can, but 'dad dancing' isn't really what they need. It's become a sort of 'wet play dance club'. I think I'll try Country Dancing for indoor P.E. one day; it's not so different from line dancing.

A field at the side of the school has become available to purchase. It's smaller than the one we lease from next door, but more easily accessible. We could use both. Tonight's governors' meeting included a discussion on whether the L.E.A. should purchase it for us. The problem with any open field in flat Lincolnshire is that on a gusty day there is no stopping the wind whipping across. The position of the new field clearly bothered Mrs. Smith, local council governor.

"So are the staff going to stand in a line breaking the wind?" she inadvisably asked.

"Well the staff usually stand on the field breaking wind!" I inadvisably replied.

There followed a tumbleweed moment. I waited a few seconds for at least a little giggle or smirk to ripple through; but silence!

I began to realise that my sense of humour and that of the governing body were parallel lines, never to meet.

* * * * * * * * * * * * * *

28

I took a 'cycling proficiency' lesson today for the children. I take them half a mile down the road to a crossroads so that they can practise right and left turns in a real situation. Although I put large boards up warning traffic that there are children cycling up ahead, some drivers ignore them.

Today a huge articulated lorry approached the junction at great speed. The 'Give Way' was not on his road, it was on the road which crossed it, so he was just going to speed through. I saw him approaching and faced him with my arm in the air. I was trusting that my high vis jacket made me look enough like a policeman to make him stop.

He slammed on his brakes, came to a halt by me and wound his window down. The bulk of the man matched the articulated lorry that he was driving. He was dressed in standard lorry driver attire – a dirty white singlet, and his tattoos were so thick on his arms and shoulders that no skin was visible. He had a shaved head and a stubbly chin.

I drew myself up to my full five foot eight height and put on my best authoritative voice.

"There are children cycling here. Do you want to kill one of them?"

"No," he said sheepishly.

"Then go slower," I declared.

"Yes – right – sorry officer!" he muttered, and pulled away, picking up speed to fifteen miles an hour.

I wonder what the penalty is for impersonating a police officer!

29

An amazing Saturday morning football match. The huge primary school with its boastful football team arrived at our tiny village school full of bravado and confidence. The confidence may have been temporarily subdued as they ran the gauntlet of headless chickens and rabid beast, but it soon returned when they reached our little dyke-lined pitch and saw that we played a girl in the team. You could visibly see their mirth and derision as they eyed-up their opposition and anticipated a 20-0 victory.

Claire wiped the smile from their faces with an amazing cross to David, who volleyed it in after five minutes. It was a tough game, but when the final whistle went, our 2-1 win was enough to see them make a quick escape back to their coach, tails between their legs, and having to wait another year for a crack at the cup.

We are in the semis!

Mr. Cook arrived to discuss the new toilet block and classroom. He assures me that there was no need for the letters, we would have got it anyway. Why am I not convinced? 'What colour did I want to paint over the duck poo?'

"Lilac," I said.

I'm now wondering if it is too late to change my mind.

As we have been planning the next residential adventure trip, our travellers' son, who lives in a caravan at the side of the road just outside the village, has not been attending school for a couple of weeks. The welfare officer was in this afternoon to discuss his non-attendance and was going to call on them later. I suggested that she tell the parents that Wayne could not join us on the trip as he had not attended school. An hour later she rang to warn me that Wayne's dad was on his way to school to flatten me.

The children had gone home at the end of school when Mr. Butcher stomped across the playground, intending to live up to his name! He was six foot one and about twenty-two stones. His biceps were like ostrich eggs. He burst into the classroom, started thumping on the top of the piano, and using abusive language.

"There's no need to be aggressive," I said.

At this point he said,

"I'm not being aggressive."

Then changed his mind!

"I am being aggressive," he shouted and gripped me round the throat, pushing me backwards, chairs and tables falling in our wake. Finally pushing me against the far wall he spluttered,

"If Wayne ain't going on that trip, you're not going on that trip. I've been to prison for GBH and I'll go again!"

I've watched enough crime dramas to know that you don't give in to terrorists.

"This isn't doing Wayne any good!" I squeaked through a constricted windpipe. Actually I was also thinking that it wasn't doing me much good either. Suddenly he let me go, and with a defeated look on his face, said,

"Well you tell me what I'm to do then."

I got him to sit on a chair made for a five year-old while I sat on a desk that was still upright, and we discussed a compromise. He sends Wayne to school every day and then Wayne comes on the trip.

Mr Butcher spat on his hand and held it out for me to shake. I shook his hand then went to the sink to wash my hands for two minutes as he waddled back across the playground.

* * * * * * * * * * * * * *

31

Indoor games today saw the introduction of Country Dancing. It had a mixed response. Many enjoyed it, but some of the boys are still at the stage of it being an embarrassing no-no to dance with a girl. If I can get them all to hold hands it will be a major breakthrough.

Amy struggles with language – mainly bad language. Whenever I've approached her mum before about Amy's or her brother's behaviour, she's not only defended them to the hilt, but positively denied that they could be anything but perfect. Today Amy told someone to go away, but not in those words; and she actually wrote the words on a piece of paper. Determined to acquire evidence this time, I looked through her work and found identical formation of three of the letters in the four-letter word. Her writing is, in fact, quite distinctive. Knowing that if I told Amy off in school, mum would be raging at the school door, I decided to call on them at home as I passed the house on my way home.

I was armed with the note and the evidence.

Amy's mum is a fearful sight to behold, even on a good day! Her look can only be described as 'anarchist Goth'. With jet black, spiky hair, 'Lone Ranger' make-up and dressed in metal-studded leather jacket and trousers, she would look more at home standing by a Harley Davison on Whitby seafront on Goth weekend. She was standing in the doorway waiting for me as I had rung to let her know I was coming.

"She didn't do it!" she growled before I told her what she had done.

As I tried to explain it, spittle and foam was appearing at the edges of her mouth, and her twisting face was becoming even more distorted than when it was still. Give me Mr. Butcher any day. Even the rabid dog next to the school was less frightening than this!

I showed her my proof.

"This is Amy's distinctive script. Look, an example of her sloping letter 'u', the same pen flick at the end of her 'c' and the little curl on the 'k'.

She almost combusted! She yelled,

"So she wrote the 'u', the 'c' and the 'k', but someone else put the other letter in front of them!"

I backed off down the path, admitting defeat. No way was I turning my back on her. I wished I'd taken that hard-bristled yard brush. I'm now at home wondering where I might get a Valium tablet to go with my double port!

* * * * * * * * * * * * * *

32

We finally set off this morning on our residential trip. Wayne has been coming to school since my 'meeting' with his dad, but didn't turn up today to set off on the trip. Thinking that I would be in big trouble when I got back if I went without him, I called on them on the way. Mr. Butcher came to the caravan door and said,

"He's bad, me duck."

Meaning, 'He's too ill to come, sir.'

So we are here without him. The camping pods we've booked are really chicken huts – wooden tents; unbelievably basic. It's three sleeping bags on the floor in each chicken hut, and I'm in one with Martin and Keith. There's a main building with toilets, showers, canteen, etc.

We climbed a steep hill this afternoon, parking the minibus in a layby part way up. I realised that when they returned down the hill it would be easy to run down and lose control, not being able to stop. As the road ran horizontally across the slope of the hill, this would be very dangerous. I suggested that they should not run back down, but if they accidentally picked up speed, they should run into the side of the minibus to stop them, and not run into the road. As we came back, Keith picked up speed! He did as I asked and crashed into the minibus. The minibus is rented, and now has a massive dent in the side. Keith has a sprained shoulder.

33

Keith moaned all night last night as his shoulder hurt, so we didn't get much sleep in our chicken hut. Out on another walk today, Melissa slipped over the steep side of a drop by the path and badly grazed her leg. Chris jumped down without injuring himself to help her back up. Along with Keith's shoulder, that's just two injuries so far – not bad really.

The activity we had this afternoon is likely to prove to be the highlight of the trip. We went gorge scrambling. This entailed walking and climbing up a dried-up stream, which when full of water, tumbles down a cliff face from a great height. The first half was relatively easy, walking and scrambling up the river bed. Then it got tricky – cliff faces that would normally be waterfalls, and we had to harness up in proper climbing gear. Each cliff face got bigger the further we went. Finally there was the 'Smartie tube'! This was a hole through the rock face that we had to squeeze through for several metres in order to come out on top. There was an opt-out, where we could choose to circumnavigate the Smartie tube and avoid the potential dangers.

Beth, of classroom tug-of-war fame, should have chosen the opt-out! She was far too big for this tube, but she desperately wanted to do it, and entered the hole at the bottom. Needless to say, she didn't emerge from the top! She reached a point where she could go no further, but as we investigated the problem, it became clear that she couldn't reverse either because she was totally stuck! Luckily Beth's a tough nut and didn't panic. There were no tears and no histrionics.

I could feel panic rising on two counts; firstly how do I tell the parents when I get back that their daughter is in a Smartie Tube, and secondly that I hadn't done a Risk Assessment for getting stuck in a Smartie tube.

After ten minutes of wriggling and shuffling she eventually emerged feet-first back at the bottom. Then, of course, she circumnavigated the tube to join us at the top to great applause.

I don't think I'll ever be able to look at a tube of Smarties again without a little shudder and a smile!

34

Colin had stomach cramps this morning, and as a doctor was in the main building seeing a member of the hostel staff, we asked him to have a quick look at him. The young doctor wondered if Colin had constipation.

"Have you defecated recently," he asked him.

I don't think he's a dad yet!

"Uh?" was Colin's reply.

The doctor tried again,

"Have you opened the stable door lately?"

Perhaps he keeps horses.

I thought I'd come to the rescue.

"Have you done a poo since getting here," I asked.

Hopefully the doctor's laxative suggestions will help.

We had a pony-trekking experience this afternoon. We were all novices, though I have ridden a few times before but not mastered the technique. My brother, who is a helper on the trip, left the horse shortly after mounting. He was thrown headfirst over the horse's head, completed a somersault, and landed on his back in front of the horse. Apart from being shaken and bruised, he's fine and continued the trek.

The leader of the trekking company was in charge. He was an older man, sergeant-major type, who bawled at the inexperienced children, and was extremely strict with us all about staying in line, not letting the horses eat leaves, etc. He even hit some children on their helmets with his riding crop. Then suddenly Matthew's horse slipped him off, but he landed gently. Five other horses then bolted, literally galloping away. This included me and my horse. None of us had the slightest control at all, and it looked distinctively like a Thelwell cartoon.

The 'sergeant-major' couldn't chase after us because he had to check that Matthew was all right. Half a mile further on the five horses came to a natural halt, the children more frightened of what the boss-man would say than the exhilarating ride. I assured them that everything would be fine. He had lost control of the group, so when he reached us with everyone else, he said not a word.

Post Script: Why is it that when horses gallop, the rider goes up as the horse goes down, and then when the horse's back comes up, the rider comes down?!?!

35

Last night it was spaghetti bolognese for tea on the final night of the trip. Martin ate too much too fast and fifteen minutes into sleep time he shot up to a sitting position in his sleeping bag, and projectile vomited. I heard it splatter down my sleeping bag! The three of us managed to clean up over the next half hour, and apart from a pervading bolognese smell, the rest of the night was uneventful.

The same could not be said about the journey home; the minibus broke down on the way back to school. A little voice from the back of the bus said,

"I think you put diesel in at the petrol station!"

The clever clogs was right; I'd filled up with diesel a mile back and the bus takes petrol. My brother hot-footed it back to the petrol station just to make sure but our nostrils had already confirmed it. Apparently petrol engines aren't keen on diesel! Fortunately we'd broken down by a pub with an adventure playground in the garden. How fortuitous was that! A breakdown truck towed the minibus to a garage where the petrol tank was emptied of diesel and refilled with petrol. The whole episode took four and a half hours. We eventually arrived back, and when I got home tonight my tea was ready - spaghetti bolognese!

I couldn't cope!

* * * * * * * * * * * * * * *

36

The new P.E. shirts have arrived and they look amazing. We tried them out in games lesson today, but it was the wrong day to do it. It was 'thunderbug day'. When I was told about 'thunderbug day' I thought it was something to do with James Bond, but it seems it is the main day in the year that certain insects appear on our school field.

Thunderbugs are blackish insects that can appear in great numbers, and they land on anything yellow because the flowers they like to land on are that colour. Not only are tennis balls yellow, but so are our new school shirts.

We all set off for the field looking smart in crisp, new yellow shirts and ran back ten minutes later in totally black shirts. Next year I want to know in advance when 'thunderbug day' is!

It was the semi-final of the football tournament today. We were finally knocked out but the team members have done themselves proud. We've finished third in the league and got as far as the semis in the cup. I'm proud of them all.

As we're approaching the end of the summer term, sports' days are looming. An area one, the date of which is fixed, and the school one which is flexible. The weather forecast this week is changeable. I hope we don't have to cancel, it's such a hassle contacting all the parents.

When we reached the end of school this afternoon, the chairs were on the desks and children were stood by them ready for home. A peaceful end to the day; in two minutes time the room would be empty and I could relax a bit. Then it happened! We have fire extinguishers on wall hooks in the classrooms because health and safety is obviously very important, but James somehow managed to dislodge the one near his desk. It crashed off its hook and landed on his foot. When full, fire extinguishers are very heavy, and James, of course was in a lot of pain. The other problem was – the appliance went off. A forceful jet of water powered into the classroom full of children. Whilst I was checking that James was all right, the appliance continued to empty, as did the classroom with the saturated members of the class making a fast exit.

No serious damage was done to James's foot – probably a bruise – but I don't know how long it will take the classroom to recover! Would foam have been better than water? Hopefully I'll never find out!

* * * * * * * * * * * * * *

The school is growing in numbers and the parents are hoping to get a minibus for the school next term to bring pupils in from surrounding villages and the nearby town. The news from Mr. Cook today is that building work on an extension, which will include more classroom space as well as toilets, will begin during the summer holiday. My altercation with the L.E.A. has paid off, but it was suggested that I don't apply for any jobs in the near future! I think I've upset a few key players. We will soon be appointing a new part-time teacher.

Today was the area sports' day. We went as a school with some parent supporters to compete with other schools. As a small school we try to include any children who want to join in. Alan is not a sporty sort of child; he can't run fast, throw well or anything else physical, really. The other day he was the other side of my desk when he suddenly disappeared. He'd fallen over for no apparent reason, and there was a dull thud. He didn't bounce in the way that most children of his age do. He wanted to take part in the sports' day so we included him. We were totally outclassed by the other schools and came last, or near to last in almost everything until the obstacle relay race. This began with running to collect a beanbag, coming back with it, putting it in a hoop and then fetching another which was a bit further away. After four beanbags there was the net to crawl under and various other obstacles to encounter. And we were winning! Three of our contestants had got a good lead on everyone else, and it was all down to the last runner. Mrs. Jones and I looked to see who it was, and at the same time, uttered,

"Alan!"

Our hopes were shattered. He set off, picked up the first beanbag and looked at it, wondering what to do with it despite watching his three team mates before him. He began to run back with it, then changed his mind and ran forwards again. Then stopped. Then turned round again and looked puzzled. The team in second place passed him, then the third. Everyone was yelling – some encouraging, some instructing, others saying what they thought of him, but Alan continued in his own little world until he came in last.

Ah well, it is what it is!

Tomorrow will be our own school sports. The weather is holding!

39

The weather was still unsettled for our sports' day today, and the forecast was sunny intervals with the chance of a thunderstorm at some point. There is the same forecast for the next few days so I decided to go for it. At 2pm we went out on to the field with the sun disappearing behind a very large, very black, cloud. The parents were all gathered to watch the spectacle – which is exactly what it was!

By 2:30 the older juniors sprint contestants were lined up at the start. Big drops of rain had just started to fall, flattening hair to heads and shirts to bodies.

"On your marks...." I yelled.

The world lit up with a stunning, vibrant flash of forked lightning.

"Get set...." I bellowed.

The loudest clap of thunder ever heard echoed around the school field.

"Go!" I roared.

The heavens opened and the rain poured down so hard it bounced a foot back up off the grass. The sprinters sprinted like they had never done before, probably breaking all records, but we don't know who won because they didn't stop after the finishing line, and the judges had already gone. I stood alone in the middle of the empty field, with everyone crowded back into the school or parents back in their cars. I tugged my sodden shirt away from my soaked body and walked slowly back to school with the field squelching beneath my feet. One of the dads watched me enter the school and called out,

"I always knew you were mad!" I think he said it in fun, but I'll never be sure.

* * * * * * * * * * * * * *

40

There were two staff interviews today, one for the part time teacher and the other for a midday controller. I got into school this morning to get ready for the interviews, but when I looked down I saw that I was wearing odd shoes. I keep them in the under stairs cupboard at home and there's no light in there. I obviously pulled out right and left shoes, but not ones that matched. It was too late to go home and come back, so odd shoes it was.

I was very tempted to have Gus do the teacher interview; I would have been interested to see if the candidates answered the ventriloquist's dummy or looked at me when they replied. In the end I decided against it – the odd shoes were probably enough for them to cope with. Mrs. Page will start in September.

The decision between the two midday controller candidates was a no-brainer. One candidate, who arrived in leathers on her motorbike with sidecar was asked,

"How do you feel about being in charge of the school over lunchtime?"

She replied, "Oh my goodness, I have enough trouble controlling my own two."

After thus shooting herself in the foot, she asked,

"Would it matter if I didn't come in every day?"

The other lady got the job!

41

Today we said goodbye to the Year 6's; their primary school days are over. We celebrated with a water fight at our little pond near to the foxes' burial site. We were all soaked but thoroughly enjoyed ourselves. There were lots of tears – not because they were wet, but because they were sad to leave. The school will be a sadder place without them, and the football team will miss Claire and David, who are both leaving. Never mind, we look forward to meeting some new four year-olds in September.

The school will continue to be a hive of activity through the summer as work starts on the extension. And hopefully the existing part of the school will have a chance to recover from the sights, smells and traumas of the past months.

September, and a new school year. The building work is well under way; we'll soon have a bit more room and indoor toilets. Yippee! There are new Reception children in, including twins – Phil and Andrew. They've not been in school long enough to sort out names yet.

"Good afternoon, Mrs. Jones," they chorused in harmony.

"I'm not Mrs. Jones," I replied.

"Good afternoon, Mrs. Watterson," they chorused again.

"I'm not MRS. Watterson," I said.

Well as they're identical twins, I'm sure they'll get my name before I get theirs.

A fence borders the playground and the dyke and Jonathan was sitting on it this afternoon, watching the playtime football game. I've not seen sitting on this fence as a potential danger before, but when one of the footballers, (I'm not sure who), kicked a ball that soared into the air, it was predestined where it was going to land. As I remember it now, a few hours later, it seemed like it was in slow motion. The trajectory of the ball was always headed for Jonathan's forehead! The ball sailed through the air in a rainbow-shaped arc. And yes, it collided with Jonathan's forehead as it was sure to do.

The action continued in slow mo as he tilted backwards, feet rising until he was airborne, and then rolling and tumbling down the dyke into the water. It wasn't deep. He was unhurt and enjoyed the accolade of applause that greeted him on his emergence.

At least Ofsted aren't here to witness the fun. We're still waiting for notification of a visit.

* * * * * * * * * * * * * *

43

We've started early rehearsals for our autumn panto – Jack and the Beanstalk. The plans are laid and I've cast it. Peter is excited to be the giant – it's his first starring role. We are going to make a massive papier mache head so he'll be looking through eye holes in the neck.

I'm joining in with informal playtime games like football and basketball. I've worked out that I can delay blowing the whistle for the end of playtime until my team's in the lead. The opposition claim it's unfair, but I'm teaching them an important lesson – life isn't fair, and they shouldn't expect it to be. I love these practical ways of getting the message across!

There's a slight delay in the building work because one of the plasterers fell off his platform in the new corridor. It was only four feet off the ground but he's broken his collarbone.

Hopefully they'll send a replacement plasterer otherwise the work will be delayed indefinitely.

* * * * * * * * * * * * * *

44

The football team isn't shaping up very well without Claire and David. We've an away match soon, so we need plenty of practice.

There was notification today that a Health and Safety inspector is calling tomorrow for a routine chat. I can't wait!

Rehearsals for the panto today have gone quite well except for Samantha. She's not managing to get any feeling into her one line at all. The giant supposedly treads on her foot. She separates every word and uses an annoying sing-song voice:

"Ow...my...toe...you've...hurt...my...toe."

I've demonstrated several times how to say it with agony in her voice, but every time without fail she sings,

"Ow...my...toe...you've...hurt...my...toe."

Oh well, it might get a laugh for the wrong reason.

My team won today's playtime football game by one goal but I had to make playtime twenty-five minutes long to get there.

45

The Health and Safety inspector arrived as planned. As we sat down opposite each other in our two metre by two metre office, head's room, staff room, I noticed within thirty seconds, the bare wires of the electric heater lying on the floor between our feet. It just needed a plug on it. In itself it wasn't dangerous; only if you stuck the wires in a socket, but my initial guilty reaction was to stamp my foot on the wires so he couldn't see them. The result was to make it more obvious, like a guilty child pretending they were innocent. He was very good about it, considering.

On the mention of a Health and Safety manual, I declared that I didn't think one had been written yet. He promised to put it in the post for me.

Today's local newspaper has sensationalised the demise of the plasterer. The headline declares,

'MAN IN PLAYGROUND PLUNGE!'

What they'll do to sell papers! It wasn't in the playground and it wasn't a plunge. The arc indented in the plaster confirmed a slow slide off the four foot platform. There were no witnesses.

Another plasterer is being sent.

Hopefully it will be a younger model, a bit steadier on his/her feet!

* * * * * * * * * * * * * * * *

46

It's Harvest Festival time and yesterday we went to the old redundant church which is now owned by the Redundant Churches Trust to clean it up for us to have our service in. This served another purpose too; we have been talking about 'the four-minute mile', and the church is exactly a mile from us, so to get the feel of what a mile is we walked there with mops, buckets, cleaning fluids, brushes, etc. And yes, it did feel like a mile! The mess in the church was horrendous. As well as all the spiders, cobwebs and dust, the floor and pews were completely covered with pigeon poo. Having spent two hours cleaning it all up we then had to walk back. I hadn't thought of that!

For the service attended by parents there today, we had prepared some songs and sketches celebrating the harvest of crops, shops, and a little diversely – factories. The mime we had prepared for factories used the children to be the mechanics of a canning process for baked beans. They did all the arm movements to illustrate what happens in the production line. I'd picked Donald to introduce the mime. He was supposed to say,

"Our machine puts baked beans into tins."

The problem is he doesn't sound many consonants, but manages all the vowels. Every time he practised it, it came out,

"Our a-ine uts a eans in-a ins."

Despite going over it multiple times it always came out the same. The parents watching hadn't a clue what the scene was about.

But that's what inclusion is all about, isn't it?

* * * * * * * * * * * * * * *

47

The away football match was a disaster; it was our turn to lose 12-0. So I thought, to cheer the team up, I would take an adventurous route home. Near to the school we visited is a small stream, and as I understood it, it is possible to drive down this shallow stream for three hundred yards and out to a ford at the other end. My car was followed by another car, a parent who had kindly helped with team transport. When she saw my car enter the 'river' she stopped her car to watch.

All went well for the first fifty yards. Some fishermen up ahead quickly wound in their lines when they saw me coming, and headed off. The engine spluttered a few times before finally giving up the struggle. Turning the key did nothing to help. Then I made my second mistake; I opened the driver's door. The stream was obviously deeper than I thought because water swirled through the open door. Children's lunch boxes and bags were floating around the back of the car. One of the girls in the team burst into tears.

Mandy, the parent from the other car, helped me to lift the children through the window and on to the tow path. She then tucked her skirt into her knickers, waded in and tried to help me push the car backwards. But it wouldn't move. A kind passer-by suggested I put the car into reverse gear and keeping turning the key. Each turn of the key made the car jump backwards.

Success! Ten minutes later we were out and the car started. We returned to school by the boring road, but we'd had an adventure, and quite forgotten the 12-0.

48

Anticipating adverse comments about yesterday's misadventure, I put a sign in the back window of my car this morning.

'River trips available by appointment with the head teacher.'

I thought a touch of humour might help, and I think it did because no-one said a word. At least, not to me!

Our local M.P. came in today to talk about the nearly completed building work. He has been instrumental in helping us get what I asked for, but I found him quite pompous. He suggested a plaque in the new toilet block with his name on it. I was tempted to suggest we put it above the boys' urinals so they had something to aim for in life. But, unusually for me, I kept my mouth shut!

* * * * * * * * * * * * *

49

Today was the Spilsby joint schools music festival. Our school isn't part of that cluster so the children weren't involved, but I was guest conductor/compere. The venue was a very large Methodist Chapel. There is a massive balcony all the way round, and the pulpit where the conductor stands is raised up very high on a level with that balcony, and the secondary school orchestra is below the pulpit. The combined primary schools, about twelve in total, sit in the main part of the chapel, with parents in the balcony. 'Bigwigs' and invited guests sit in the gallery behind the pulpit.

As my ventriloquism skills have gained in confidence, I used Gus to introduce some songs and to entertain. Naughty Gus managed to fall out of the pulpit and drape himself over the head of one of the orchestra players. At least he didn't land in a euphonium or similar.

The highlight was 'Raindrops Keep Falling on my Head'. I took a loaded water pistol with me, left the pulpit, and ran amok. It was a panto-type moment. Imagine my delight when I saw one of the L.E.A. bigwigs wearing a shiny suit behind the pulpit within firing range! I pointed the pistol at him with a glint in my eyes. There was a look in his that I interpreted as panic – or threat – or both. Taking pity on him I made sure the water didn't quite reach him. After all, he'd given up his evening to support the event. The least I could do was let him go home dry.

The success - or not - of my participation in the event will be revealed when I get asked - or not - to do next year's.

* * * * * * * * * * * * * *

50

The new block is open for use. The official opening will be in a few days' time with the new Chair of the Education Committee. We have to put on a bit of entertainment. I am informed that this is usually the school choir singing a song or reciting some poems, giving readings, etc. But I have other ideas!

I now have my own office. I have put a large, blue, bouncy inflatable armchair in it. It makes quite a disgusting sound when you sit down. More fun! I was sitting in it today when Peter entered. Peter has some particular problems, autistic related. He was in trouble but didn't want to hear what I said to him. He closed the door and immediately covered both ears with his hands. Every time I opened my mouth to speak he bent over backwards like a limbo dancer, hands still over his ears. He's remarkably flexible. The top half of his body ended up horizontal so that he was staring at the ceiling. When he started singing and humming to drown out anything I might say, the whole event looked like a circus act.

I eventually dismissed him, still not sure what his misdemeanour was. I think he had suffered enough, and I had been suitably entertained. His mum says he's got a plectrum. I don't think he plays guitar; I reckon she's confusing it with spectrum.

Tomorrow's the performance of Jack and the Beanstalk at last.

51

The panto was a resounding success today with one exception. It was supposed to be an amusing moment when Graham pulled the giant's trousers down. Peter had red and yellow spotted shorts on underneath his trousers and over his underpants. I was sitting at the piano and decided to watch the audience's faces during the trouser drop. When the moment came, the smiles and giggles didn't happen. Instead, there were gasps of shock, mouths opened and eyebrows lifted. I turned to look at the stage. Peter, in his huge papier mache head, was desperately trying to pull up his pants, shorts and trousers as the mischievous Graham had yanked down the lot! Although there were lots of entertaining moments in the performance, the Full Monty experience was the main talking point.

Thank goodness Ofsted were not in!

52

Today was the grand opening of the new block. The lady who is the new Chair of the Education Committee, duly arrived to do her duty. The programme was: Entertainment by the children, Head teacher speech, Official opening by the Chair. The room was packed as many parents turned up to join the children, staff and governors for the exciting event. In place of normal entertainment, the older children had practised some comedy sketches. We did a very funny sketch with a row of four cowboys in a line pretending to be riding horses, and passing messages up and down the line to tell the one at the end that he has an arrow stuck in his leg. Then there was a crazy sketch called 'McGinty's Dead', but the highlight was a mime to the song 'Mahna Mahna', made famous by The Muppets. Hannah was amazing imitating the very deep voice of the lead singer. The backing group were equally entertaining. None of this was relevant in any way, but was better than someone reading a boring poem or playing the wrong notes on a recorder. I'm not sure the Chair appreciated the humour – it wasn't what she was expecting.

Gus had sat patiently on my knee throughout, but he came to life when it was my turn. Eyeballing the V.I.P. as he passed her to get to the front, he said,

"Who's she?"

"She's the Chair of the Education Committee," I replied.

"She's a chair?..?" Gus was surprised. "Can I sit on her?"

There was a ripple of amusement around the room, but again I felt the humour was lost on our guest. She forced the sides of her mouth to turn up, pretending a smile, but it never reached her eyes.

* * * * * * * * * * * * * * *

53

Karen fell over in the playground yesterday. She hurt her shoulder, but by the end of school she seemed fine. Her mother came in today wondering why I hadn't let her know that her daughter had broken her collarbone. Apparently, they'd been at the hospital until late. I asked her when she'd taken her to the hospital and she said it was when she realised there was something wrong around 8pm.

"So if you didn't know she had a painful injury until 8pm, how was I to know at 3pm?" I asked.

Amazingly, she accepted this as a logical explanation and went away quite happy. I, on the other hand, am wondering what sort of jinx is on the school for broken collarbones. That's three if you count the 'man in playground plunge'.

We're celebrating our music lessons with a performance of Samson and Delilah tomorrow.

It's a set of songs with some added drama during the singing, and a narrator. Parents will hopefully attend at the end of the afternoon to listen to the Bible story of how Samson loses his amazing strength because his hair is cut off, and regains it when he grows it back. The climax is when he pulls down the pillars holding up the roof of a pagan temple. I'm going to use one of our amazing auditorium maroons to give the crash. I'm looking for how to make it safer!

54

Breaking news! Ofsted are coming in a couple of days' time. I can't wait! I've been asking Mrs. Jones for her planning, but she always has an excuse. Today, with even more urgency, I said I needed it. She told me it had been stolen from the boot of her car. If someone was going to steal from the boot of her car, it wouldn't be her lesson plans they were interested in; what sad person would do that? I saw panic on her face. For some reason she's worried about the state of her class stockroom; apparently it's untidy. I would say that is the least of our worries.

I decided to put the maroon for today's performance of Samson and Delilah in a new chrome pedal bin. I thought that would be strong enough, and just to make sure, I wedged the bin between the piano and the wall. Helen was responsible for pressing the switch on the wall socket to activate it. Chris was standing near the piano, narrating. At the exact moment of Samson pulling the pillars in and collapsing the roof, I nodded to Helen and she pressed the switch. As I thought, the resounding crash temporarily deafened everyone present. Smoke was pouring in clouds from behind the piano and the lid of the new pedal bin came flying over the top of the piano and hit Chris on the head. For a couple of seconds it was a bit like a scene in an apocalypse film.

I think there was a stunned silence – I'm not sure, because I had also gone deaf – until I shouted to the children, "Sing!" and continued to play. I was told I looked like a mad professor at the piano with smoke coming out of my hair and ears, but the show must go on! The children's response was magnificent. Another successful performance, and Chris was almost unhurt.

55

After school today, Friday, I went into Mrs. Jones's classroom to see if she was ready for Monday's Ofsted, and had any planning for me. The scene that greeted me was one of total chaos. She had emptied her stockroom out into the classroom to sort it and tidy it. Every available space in the room was covered with some sort of debris. She must have seen the shock on my face.

"Don't worry, I'm living here over the weekend," she assured me.

I didn't even mention planning.

56

Today, Monday morning – Ofsted Day 1, I arrived at 8am to find the inspectors already in school, and a note from Mrs. Jones saying she was ill and not coming in. At least she had cleared her classroom over the weekend and put it all back in the stockroom. But she hadn't left any planning! We managed to organise a brave supply teacher at extremely short notice, and I took the infant class for the first lesson in order to give her a little time to plan something for the rest of the day. The timetabled lesson was R.E. and with no planning I taught it on the hoof. The inspector who came to watch the lesson just happened to be the R.E. adviser for the county!

The rest of the day has passed in a haze, but I think we've done all right, all things considered!

57

At the beginning of the day – Ofsted day 2 – I used Gus to help me with the morning assembly. The lady who is leading the inspection came in to watch. Gus behaved terribly as usual. The children found him really funny like they normally do, but occasional glances in her direction gave nothing away. At the end of the assembly, the staff and children filed out, leaving her just sitting there. There was a silence in the room until she got up, came towards me, lookeme in the eyes and declared,

"You're mad!"

That was the sum total of the assembly feedback. Do I take it that she enjoyed it – or hated it – or....?

Well I'm going to view it as a positive.

The final feedback on the inspection at the end of the day is a 'satisfactory'. Considering more than a third of the teaching staff was absent, I'll take that.

Other good news today is that the minibus the parents want us to lease is all going ahead and will be delivered to the school, complete with our school name emblazoned down the side, at the beginning of next term.

* * * * * * * * * * * * * *

58

I was a few minutes late into school today. My daughter, Liz, had entered me into a competition for being the maddest dad in the area. This was being sponsored by a local newspaper, and Liz had sent in some of the school's adventures, like when we drove down the stream after the football match. We won the competition and I had to do a trolley dash in a large supermarket prior to them opening for the day. We ended up with an amazing amount of stuff, and Liz was given what must be the biggest Toblerone in the world. It is valued at about a hundred times the cost of a normal one. Having fun in school can pay off in more ways than one.

Christmas is approaching and we are making decorations and preparing our final production of the year – a nativity play. I've decided to join in again. I'll be Herod; it'll give me a chance to be aggressive.

After school today I experimented with the maroons as they appear to be a bit dangerous. There are some very heavy, solid steps up on to our stage, so when everyone had gone I put a maroon in a biscuit tin, sellotaped the lid down, and placed it under the steps which I actually struggle to even move. At the other end of the room I had the wire and switch. In the empty room the sound was catastrophic on the ears; the steps actually moved and the biscuit tin was blown apart with miniscule bits of sellotape splattered on the underside of the steps. It needs rethinking over the weekend.

59

It's Saturday, so no school today but I further experimented with the maroons. I bought a metal container from the nearby town's market. It was from the Army and Navy Stores stall, and was designed for keeping unexploded shells in. I thought this would do the trick. I put the maroon in the metal case and did up the clasp. After placing it down the bottom of the garden and bringing the wire up to the house, I activated the explosion. The metal box was destroyed, the cable snaked through the air and landed fifteen feet away from it. I think I shouldn't use them again.

Tomorrow, Sunday, is a Christingle service at the school's local Church and quite a few of our children are going. I think I'll tag along and support.

60

How do I begin to describe the events of the Christingle service? I took Mrs. Fuller, our teaching assistant, as she also wanted to give her support. The children paraded up the aisle with lighted candles stuck in decorated oranges. It was a lovely service up to the beginning of the second hymn when the vicar announced that Mr. Watterson, the head teacher of the local primary school would be giving the talk directly after the hymn.

I felt my extremities go cold as my blood decided to protect my main organs. Talk! What talk?

"I didn't know about this!" I silently mouthed to Mrs. Fuller.

Then a vague remembrance seeped into my brain. About three weeks before, the vicar had asked me as he went out of the school door one day. I'd said yes and then not given it another thought. I wanted the floor to open up and swallow me; the idea of standing in front of a church full of people, opening my mouth and nothing coming out was awful. Options came to mind:

1) Feign stomach cramps and run for the door.
2) I was on the end of a pew near a side aisle – I could drop to my knees and crawl silently past the back pews, out of the door, pretending I wasn't there at all.
3) I could improvise! After all, I'd done it for Ofsted not long ago.

By this time, the first verse was over and there were only two left. The only real choice was option 3. By the end of verse 3 my brain was up and running and I headed to the front of the church hoping that my legs didn't give way and that my tongue didn't get stuck.

I understand it went well. No-one, except for Mrs. Fuller, was any the wiser. Or so I'm told!

Was everyone just being kind?

Will Mrs. Fuller blackmail me?

Will I ever attend another Christingle service?

??????????****************??????????

61

I decided to cycle into school today, but this was a mistake because there was some black ice around. As I reached the school gate, the bike and I parted company. I entered the school grounds on my backside. Tom was just walking in to the school grounds at the same time. He heard the noise of the bike and me also entering, dramatically. He glanced across and then back, continuing on with no reaction whatsoever. I would have expected,

"Are you all right, Mr. Watterson?"

Or a fit of giggles at the sight. But nothing at all!

Fortunately I was physically unhurt; I had to become King Herod this afternoon for the nativity play. It wouldn't have looked good if I ended up back in hospital.

For my use in the play, I had fashioned a silver goblet from a plastic cup and tinfoil. My servants brought me the news that a new king had been born in Israel, and after they left I did an Oscar-winning performance of anger; shouting,

"I am the only king in Israel!"

At the same time I threw the cup behind me with great ferocity. Just like the trajectory of the football knocking Jonathan off the fence and into the dyke, I could see the trajectory of the cup heading inexorably for the closed window.

Yes, it was on target and smashed straight through the glass. My initial reaction was that I would be in trouble with the head teacher. Then I remembered that I am the head teacher! So, there are some perks to the job.

The final stable tableau was set, with all the cast assembled in usual format – Mary and Joseph behind the manger with doll; shepherds and Kings arranged behind them with animals at the side; and the back row of innocent-looking angels. Joy, one of the four year-old angels obviously got bored or tired of standing, and put her leg over the shoulder of the shepherd in front of her. It sort-of spoilt the peaceful idyll of the scene, but was well-worth it for the laugh.

62

The Health and Safety manual finally turned up in the courier post today. I think the inspector had forgotten to send it earlier in the term. I wondered if there was a chapter on head teachers smashing windows by throwing cups through them. Or maybe not cycling on black ice. I decided to have a ten minute browse through at lunchtime, but I managed to spill my hot coffee all over it.

The local country club round the other side of the village had prepared a party for our children today. This, I thought, would be great for me as I only needed to get the children there and then sit back and watch. When we arrived the floor was covered with a hundred balloons. Apparently this was their idea of planning a party. They had food prepared for an hour's time, but the children immediately jumped on the balloons – quite naturally – and burst all one hundred in two minutes. Then they stood around wondering what to do next. The country club staff mysteriously disappeared.

So I had to run an hour of party games after all. I did The Old Ford Car, which was an immediate hit. The children sit in two lines facing each other, each with a car part name such as '*engine*', listen to the story, and race round the chairs whenever their part is mentioned. We followed this with 'Winkie' and a couple of other games up to food time. I don't think we'll bother coming here again, we could have played these games in school.

When we got back there was smoke, or it could have been steam, coming off the Health and Safety manual which was drying on the radiator. I decided it would be safer to bin it.

It's a hazard that you don't need in schools.

Finally, the year has ended. Michael, the parent I had met on my first day, looked round the door after school, and a little flurry of light snow drifted past his head.

"M....m....m....Merry Christmas. It's going to b...b...be a c...c...cold one," he said.

I opened my mouth – and then closed it. I wasn't going to be caught out like that again.

"And a merry Christmas to you too," I said after a moment collecting myself.

I've looked back through this journal and there seems to be some recurring themes. Top of the list for a School Development Plan next year will be to obtain a new Health and Safety manual. Pantomime year is done, so I think we will concentrate on mini-musicals next year. There's a great one I've got in mind about a French cockerel called Chanticleer. Paul will be great in the part.

I've a residential trip in mind to *The Wharf Shed* in Derbyshire. A proper hostel; I think we'll forget barges and chicken huts!

There's been a lot of performing, a lot of learning and a lot of fun. And......we've all survived.

I'd call that a result!

About the Author

Following more than twenty-five years as a Lincolnshire head teacher, David has continued and developed his work with puppets. For the last sixteen years he has toured the UK with what is now a collection of over two hundred puppets, including Gus, running entertaining, interactive story-telling workshops in primary schools. To date he has visited three hundred and seventy-seven schools, some many times over, and worked with approximately forty-five thousand children.

Other books:

The Mysterious Case of the Mysterious Case.

A very unusual interactive book, this is a short story with forty-eight alternative versions. It is aimed at Y5 and Y6 pupils, and encourages them not only to explore the different routes a story can take, but to encourage and develop their own thinking and creative writing.

The Amazing Adventures of a Small School

One hundred years ago, on 15 June, the headteacher of a tiny Lincolnshire primary School disappeared with a Viking artefact. Fifty years later to the day, the headteacher of the same school also disappeared without trace. Fifty more years on, will the current head disappear? Is there any truth in the rumour of a hidden cellar under the school? The mysterious secrets of the school are investigated and an amazing roller-coaster of events takes the little community to the mystical and beautiful islands of Orkney. Little do they realise that this adventure will encourage them on to even more mystery and danger.

Bertie's Big Splash

This is a picture story book for five and six year olds, with illustrations by Paul Watterson, David's brother. Bertie Bullfrog is a big show-off, and the other residents of Pinker's Pond want to teach him a lesson. On Sports Day, when it comes to his best event, the Long Jump, they have a surprise waiting for him. Join the fun and see what happens to Bertie in this entertaining story.

Once Upon a Different Time

Characters from traditional stories give their version of events, and children are encouraged to develop their own creative skills. Y3 - Y6 is the target group.

David can be contacted at the following e-mail:

sueandthepuppetman@gmail.com

Copyright: D.Watterson July 2020